Turning Point: Answering the Entrepreneur's Call

Six Highly Effective Ways to Jumpstart Your Dream

Gwendolyn D. Wilson

Copyright 2017 Gwendoly D. Wilson

All rights reserved. No part of this book may be reproduced or transmitted in any form or by any means without written permission from the author.

Dedication

Special dedication and thanks to my wonderful village for your love, support and encouragement.

In honor of my mom who was my number one fan. I truly miss you. She taught us to embrace the power of love, faith and a united family.

In memory of a legacy of faith and strength from my beloved grandmother, Arlene Craft, Aunt Grace and Uncle Bill. To Aunt Betty who constantly reminds me of my childhood desire for business and money as she sings my nickname to this very day. Thank you for constantly speaking words of empowerment, purpose and motivation into my life. Your contribution will always be a part of my existence.

To my sister Melva J. McGlen, an entrepreneur in her own right, thanks so much for your inspiration, encouragement, loving and constant push to write this book.

To my brother, Gary Hart, thank you for your reserve leadership. While I studied finance and accounting; you mastered the art of financial wisdom.

To my pastor, mentor and sister, Dr. Paulette L. Scott, a very special thank you for your love, wisdom, knowledge and spirit of excellence; for always believing in me and supporting my dreams no matter what.

A loving thanks to my circle of sisters and lifelong friends, Nannie L. Johnson, Terrie V. Matthews and my cousin, Joann B. Johnson for allowing me to share my dreams and visions; and always responding with great encouragement and support.

Last but not least to Dr. Mildred Musgrove, my editor and an amazing educator; my sincerest thanks for your dedication to excellence and professionalism. Thank you for your love, insight and positive twist on everything.

Life wouldn't be the same without my village. Thank you for allowing me to be real. We have weathered many storms together and celebrated lots of victories.

The best is yet to come!

Since I was little, I've had that vision of a business woman inside me.

Thalia

Table of Contents

Introduction 1

Step One – *Believe and Walk by Faith* 9

Step Two – *Make the Decision* 30

Step Three – *Overcome Obstacles* 45

Step Four – *Write the Vision* 67

Step Five – *Execute Your Plan* 78

Step Six – *Plan to Succeed* 85

Conclusion 89

NOTES 93

Introduction

You were put on this earth to achieve your greatest self, to live out your purpose, and to do it courageously.
Dr. Steve Maraboli

Success is knowing your purpose in life, growing to reach your maximum potential, and sowing seeds to benefit others.
John C. Maxwell

"For everything there is a season and a time for every purpose under the heaven... a time to plant, a time to reap...a time to build and a time to stop working." Ecclesiastes 3:1. Every crossroad is a point in your life when you must make an important decision. At each turning point, you can either decide to seize the moment, take a leap of faith, standstill or move backward. The choice is absolutely yours and yours alone. Standing at a crossroad or a defining moment in life may be difficult. In fact, it may be the life changing season of renewal that defines your purpose.

The author believes we were born to fulfill our distinctively unique purpose in life. Within each of us is the ability to create, build and transform. You will solve problems that will change lives and the world. She firmly believes that we can learn from one another mistakes and successes. Our journey is full of challenges, victories, failures, regrets and successes. When we dare to share our story to help others we prevent detours to someone's destiny. Our stories can empower, strengthen and help others from facing the pitfalls and obstacles that we encountered on our road to destiny. How we perceive our turning points or crossroads will impact our decisions and outcome.

What is a turning point? It is a time at which a decisive change in a situation occurs, especially one with favorable results. A turning point may be a crossroad, decisive moment, crisis, moment of truth or landmark. It is a pivotal season when a significant shift occurs that propels you into your destiny. A turning point can be exciting and devastating yet many have caused some of the greatest visionaries to gift us with amazing discoveries, products and services. A turning point is a moment in time, a twinkling in life when you must change direction to fulfill your purpose. It is an awakening when clarity drives your energy, passion, and power towards your calling.

Gwendolyn defines a turning point as the breaking of a new day because it yields a fresh start and unlimited potential. There is something so refreshing and energizing about the breaking of dawn. The possibilities, opportunities and choices we can make could be life changing. Like the beginning of a new season, a new day brings forth a second chance, a rebirth and a crossing over. There is a burst of expectation with every new beginning. Each new day brings renewal, promise and empowerment to meet the demands and challenges of life. Making the decision to answer the entrepreneur's call may indeed be one of those challenges.

Do you have a dream? Is this your season? Are you an aspiring entrepreneur? Do you desire to build your dream business? Are you in transition – are you a laid-off professional? Are you longing for your dream career? Maybe you are not sure that you have a dream. Seeking to generate multiple streams of income? If your answer to any of these questions is "yes" then this book is for you. C.S. Lewis says "you are never too old to set another goal or dream a new dream". Nor are you too young to start building today.

What is the entrepreneur's call? It is a gifting, passion or longing to build or create something from nothing. The desire to offer innovative services and goods that provide solutions to change people lives. For some, your entrepreneur's call may be a life-long dream of business ownership. The entrepreneur's call may be defined as the fulfillment of your destiny and purpose. For an enthusiastic visionary, it is the beaconing to design the invention of your dreams; and for the laid-off career professional, it is the pursuit of becoming your own boss. The entrepreneur's call is the movement from passion to possibility and from vision to fruition. For most, the entrepreneurial spirit is a powerful yearning to achieve or make something great in your lifetime. It is an unfulfilled hunger to achieve your life's purpose and dream. The call is alive; the call is real. Every call demands a response. Is your call compelling you to do something different? Dare to follow your passion, answer the call.

What are the expert sayings? Entrepreneurship is growing by leaps and bounds. Women, baby boomers and millennial are making great strides in building successful businesses. Forbes states that "What's good for women is good for the economy. Economists and academics agree women entrepreneurs are an under-tapped force that can rekindle economic expansion. Women are becoming more entrepreneurial. Women owned 36% of all businesses, according to the 2012 U.S. Census – a jump of 30% over 2007."

Older Americans are increasingly launching new ventures. In fact, "2015 data from the Kauffman Foundation show that boomers were nearly twice as likely to plan to launch businesses as their millennial counterparts. The research group's 2016 Index of Startup Activity shows that those ages 55 to 64 represent 24.3 percent of all new entrepreneurs, compared to just 14.8 percent in the same age group in 1996."

"...Baby boomers are the most powerful entrepreneurial group, giving up retirement for career number 2 (or 3, 4 and so on) choosing entrepreneurship instead of retiring. The American Dream never ends, and baby boomers are finding that they are in the perfect position to build their own business."

In short, the experts are saying this is a profitable and exciting season for women, baby boomers and millennial. If there is something you always wanted to do, seize the moment, just do it. Is this your season? The author grew up during a time when our parents told us to get a good education and a good job. We were expected to work hard, do well and retire after 55. At a young age, she got the impression that it was all over after 50 or retirement. Well, she is so excited to be part of a great movement that celebrates an evolving life after 50. Today, baby boomers are changing lives by building amazing businesses and creating innovative products worldwide. Who said life begins at 50 – indeed it does!

Gwendolyn has always desired to build multiple businesses and inventions. She has created her second small business and knows firsthand the tragedy not seizing the moment when you allow procrastination to rule. Throughout her life, statistics have proven that there are others just like her who have dreamt for years about building, creating and making a difference yet have failed to launch their dream business because of hindrances and distractions. As an enthusiastic team-oriented visionary, she is compelled to challenge you to follow your dreams to completion.

Like many baby boomers, she has embraced her entrepreneurial spirit and the opportunities it yields. This book is full of her personal insight and quotes from many successful entrepreneurs and leaders. Yes, we still dream big and bold. Recapture your youthful creativity and build the business of your dream. Today, boomers continue to evolve, turning dreams and visions into reality. Join the movement, dare to move from thinking to doing!

You should read this book - If you have an unfulfilled dream. Or perhaps you did not know you actually had a dream; but you feel that there is more to life. If there is a yearning, a nagging in your heart that there is something else you must do. You believe that you are an entrepreneur with a dream. You believe there is still a longing to do more. Does the hunger to do greater continue to fill your heart?

When you are predestined to do something – build or create something amazing – your passion never goes away. This passion is your driving force which leads you to your purpose. It hungers for fulfillment. It longs for the manifestation of the dream within you. Is your genuine and distinctive ability, talents and power longing for the creation, innovation and business that will change you and the lives you touch?

Rise, shine – a new dawn is awaking; it is your turning point towards a new lifestyle and fulfillment of your dream. Your purpose is beckoning, calling you to leap forth and take action. What would happen if you built it? What problems will you solve? Whose life will be changed?

Have you ever wondered what if? What if Thomas Edison had not invented the incandescent light bulb or the phonograph? What if Nelson Mandela had not fought for freedom? What can you change? Who can you help? What will happen if you do nothing? What will be undone? Can you imagine how amazing it will be living your purpose? What footprints will you leave for others to follow?

You have a purpose in life to fulfill. You were born with a purpose driven passion to be fulfilled by only your authentic power. Are you at a turning point? Are you ready to transform your dream into a reality? If your answer is yes, follow the six highly effective steps to jumpstart your dream. Pursue your passion; just do it!

Step One – Believe and Walk by Faith

It is absolutely impossible to fulfill or accomplish anything without faith. Faith is the fuel that makes your dream a reality. Believe by definition means *to accept (something) as true; feel sure of the truth of something.* "Now faith is the reality of what is hoped for, the proof of what is not seen." Hebrews 11:1 If you chose to believe in your dreams, you must accept the dreams as true (as factual, valid and <u>real</u>). According to that definition of faith, if you hope to build a business one day, you must believe that it is a reality now; before you build it. You must believe it before you actually see it.

How do we walk by faith? Believe the dream is possible. Believe the dream is real Believe that you can become the entrepreneur you dreamed of. Put your faith in action. Every Olympian dreams of winning the gold and works to achieve that dream. Believe, focus and do it. Act like a winner and do the work required to win. As simple as it sounds for many of us, it is still not easy. But it is possible.

Believe is an inward, core response to what you perceive as truth. When you walk (move or act) out your belief, you walk by faith. Walk by faith signifies motion based on your belief. Walking is exercise. Walking is faith in action. Walking is work. Belief without action is dormant. To walk by faith exercises your beliefs until they are physically real. Faith walking makes the virtual a reality. It makes the invisible, real.

How often do you discuss, share and think about your dream; yet, it has not materialized? You believe and want to fulfill it; but, you have not added any action to your faith to move forward. Faith reveals possibilities while work (action) manifests realities. Dare to believe in the possibilities. Dare to believe in the dream. Dare to believe in you! Only when you truly believe in something can you act with purpose.

The human spirit is amazing. When you truly believe in something and you choose to act intentionally on your belief – things happen. Walking by faith is a powerful source. If you can believe it, you can achieve it. When you add action to your vision, the dream becomes alive. **Faith + work = a tangible vision.**

> *"Vision without action is merely a dream.*
> *Action without vision just passes time.*
> *Vision with action can change the world."*
> Joel A. Baker

It is not enough to just believe. You were created to produce. Work is the effort required to perform the necessary tasks to bring about your dreams. Work is the labor invested to be successful. Success does not just happen. Work, perform, succeed – you are simply, the one responsible for directing your destiny. You must choose to pursue it. What you do and think will determine your outcome.

Your belief system, attitude, thoughts, habits, and actions determine your success. Success is not an accident. It is an intentional achievement that results from hard work. It is victory over obstacles. Your success is governed by your daily life – what do you believe? What do you do? To be victorious, you must believe in you. Nothing will work if you do not believe in it. Nothing will grow until you plant the seed by faith and water it with works. Remember, it is not enough to just believe. You must act upon your faith. Believing that you can ride a bike is good. If you never get on the bike, it is futile. Getting on the bike is a must. Crashing, falling and hitting bumps are part of the course. Now, enjoy the ride and follow your path.

Believe and walk by faith is the first step to progressively fulfilling your dream. In order to walk by faith and build your dream, you must solidify your belief in both the dream and yourself. Many of you are saying "I really believe in myself and the dream; that is not the problem". Often in transitional or defining moments in life; self-doubt, discouragement and even fear challenges our faith. During these times, we have to encourage ourselves and press a little harder to motivate ourselves for the journey ahead. Like our Olympians, we must mentally, physically and totally prepare ourselves (mind, body, soul and spirit) for the task ahead to ensure victory.

To fortify our tenacity, we have provided some guidance for building up your action-driven faith along with affirmations to help you move forward towards your goals. Let us move continuously from faith to action.

A passionate belief in your business and personal objectives can make all the difference
Between success and failure. If you aren't proud of what you're doing,
Why should anybody else be?
Richard Branson

1. Believe in Yourself

You are fearfully and wonderfully made. In you are seeds of greatness. Believe in your greatness. You were created to dream dreams, see visions, produce, build, imagine and solve problems. Believe in your distinctive power. You are unique and only you can fulfill your destiny. Your dreams, passions, habits, pain, love and hope make you unequivocally unique. Despite the many challenges that you may face, your purpose is uniquely yours. Be yourself no matter what other people think. You are responsible for your own victories, successes and failures. Own it.

Believing in oneself is to live on purpose. Live with a purpose to win. To believe in yourself is to deliberately be the best "you" possible. Be your best self and invest in "You". Believe in yourself. Have faith in your abilities. Believe in yourself and the power of your dreams, even if others doubt your capabilities. Listen to your inner voice and block the negative voices. You must have an unwavering belief in your dream/vision. Unfaltering faith in you and your dream will lead you to your greatness. The only person that can stop your greatness is you.

Every man and woman is born into the world to do something unique and something distinctive and if he or she does not do it, it will never be done.
Benjamin Mays

If you think you are an entrepreneur in your heart, then you are one. Belief is the beginning of visualization "you gotta see it before you see it". As a visionary, dreamer, and innovator, you must be your #1 cheerleader. *"I think I can, I think I can"* while moving forward said the little engine that could. Remember Step One – believe and walk in your faith. Think like a winner. Believe like a winner. Act like a winner.

"As a man thinks in his heart, so is he." Proverbs 23:7. As an entrepreneur, see yourself as an Olympian who continues to evolve. The Olympics represent people from all walks of life - every nationality, gender and creed. Each individual enters the stage (life) as a potential winner. Olympians work hard and train to be the best. They take responsibility for their successes and failures. They own it against all odds. They believe in their ability to compete as they prepare to win. They simply train to succeed.

> *I believe there's an inner power that makes winners or losers. And the winners are the ones who really listen to the truth of their hearts.*
> Sylvester Stallone

Whatever you really believe in, you invest time, energy and money in it. If you truly believe in yourself, you must invest in you - educate you and train you to be your best self. You must believe not only in your ability to evolve into the entrepreneur or whatever you desire to do; you must also believe in the dream.

Most Olympic winners, see themselves as winners even before they win. They act by faith – they train, work hard and visualize their reality in advance. They employ coaches, mentors and other professionals to support their dream; they create a dream team. Do not be afraid to ask for help. Olympic athletes train with other dreamers (athletes) and compete to win at various levels with the ultimate goal in mind. They constantly challenge themselves and take risks. Athletes work harder, climb higher, overcome obstacles – constantly moving forward reaching for the gold. To succeed you must have a winner's mindset and do the work required to win.

Stop doubting yourself, work hard, and make it happen.
Anonymous

2. Believe in your Dream

You must believe not only in yourself and your ability to evolve into the entrepreneur you have always dreamed of being. You must believe in the Dream from conception to completion, believe every step of the way. You must accept the Dream as a reality and actively work your faith and create a plan of action to accomplish the necessary steps from start to finish. There is a distinct difference in having a desire for something to work versus committing to its success. As the visionary, you must be the believer/navigator – the one who believes in the vision and navigates the path to reality with all of its possibilities and obstacles.

    a. <u>**Visualize it.**</u> Mentally build it. Do the work, research your potential client base and target markets. Once you add action, the dream transforms into a vision. See what others are doing. Think about what makes your vision, product and services unique. Devote yourself to it. Analyze the vision and mission. What do you want to accomplish? What do you want to build? What problem(s) will you solve? "If you build it, they will come."

Believing in your dream means you must yield to your Passion. Yield to what excites you about the dream – what you desire to create. Perhaps, like me, you desire to see others that are stuck and at a crossroad in life make the leap into their desired future. Are you stuck in your dream or business? Do you desire to make a change? Do you struggle with fear, procrastination and doubt? Yet, the vision, the dream is ever before you – your passion and enthusiasm to build continues to speak to you. To win in life and business you have to have a winner's mindset.

Winners, I am convinced, imagine their dreams first.
They want it with all their heart and expect it
to come true. There is, I believe, no other way to live.
Joe Montana

b. **_Pursue it!_** Make it your priority. Choose to win. Get started now. The initial step to overcoming the fear of failure is to believe you can win and just do it. Remember, failure is not fatal. Nor is failure your only option. Success is always a viable option when you believe.

When you make the dream a priority – there must be an urgency to build. Make plans. Set objectives and timelines. Pursuing the dream should be of utmost importance. Reevaluate your top priorities. The execution of your dream should be in the top three. Justify the reason for its rank in your life.

Ask yourself, will it make my family life better? Then give the dream priority treatment and attention to change your future.

Believe in yourself, believe in your dream. The biggest difference between successful people and unsuccessful people is not intellect, opportunity or resources; it is the belief that they can make it happen. Successful people believe that they can make their goals a reality. You will deal with uncertainty, failure and vulnerability. You must trust that if you move forward anyway, you will figure it out along the way.

Trust your instincts. Trust yourself. Take risks. Do not take "no" for an answer. Do not look back. Look forward. Dream bigger dreams!

c. *Analyze it!* Perform a SWOT analysis on your dream business. Analyze the strengths, weaknesses, opportunities and threats of starting your particular business, invention or endeavor. Devote sufficient efforts to start right and start strong. Do the research; perform due diligence. Determine what makes your business, services and/or products unique, then optimize it. Reach out to mentors, partner with others to learn, grow and empower yourself. Strive to be the best. Immerse yourself in learning daily.

3. Put Your Faith to Work

Believing in yourself and your dream is essential to fulfilling your future and destiny. It is impossible to pursue your dream without believing that you are capable of meeting the challenge. Success will not happen overnight, it will require hard work, dedication and determination. The inevitable short cut or easy road may not be a part of your journey. Ask yourself – am I willing to put in the hard work necessary to obtain my goals? If you want others to believe and invest in you and your dream; then you must be the first to invest and believe in you and your dreams.

Believe you have everything you need. Embrace it, it is already in you. Quiet that small voice of doubt inside and believe with your whole heart. Stop worrying. Stop criticizing yourself. Give yourself and your dream a chance.

Pause; take an assessment of your abilities. Commit. Say yes to your dream. Decide you are worth the investment. Say yes to the dream and plan to evolve.

    a. *Assess what you have already accomplished in life.* Successful sole proprietor raised a family, managed a team/division, remarkable career, educational accomplishments, outstanding leader, overcame life challenges... Remember, as a working professional, you had great ideas, solved problems, created and implemented plans that helped your employers succeed. Now it's your turn. So feel good about what you have already accomplished and continue to dream big. Celebrate your accomplishments and recognize you have the potential to accomplish greater. Make a list of your past accomplishments. Now make a list of your future accomplishments and goals. Dare to dream big, courageous and without limit. Trust yourself.

Believe you can and are capable of growing. Believe you can build a thriving enterprise. To embrace the entrepreneur's spirit and build a prosperous entity does not mean that you have to establish a multi-million-dollar company like Apple but you can if you want to. Nothing is impossible.

Most successful entrepreneurs are not overnight wonders. Although it may happen to some, it is not the norm. The majority of business owners build over time drawing from their attributes, strengths, failures and opportunities of the past to create a better future. Knowing what you are made of and have accomplished guides your future. Experience is truly a great teacher. Continue to grow and evolve from your past experiences, successes and failures to explore new possibilities and reach for greater heights.

In order to succeed, we must first believe that we can.
Nikos Kazantzakis

b. *<u>Commit to the vision, dream or whatever you believe you want to accomplish.</u>* When you commit to anything, you must actively obligate yourself to making it happen. Commitment requires you to dedicate your time, effort and resources to fulfill the vision. Designate quality time to think about the plan. Think big. Think bold. Then make the decision to develop, build or create something; you must be devoted it. You must be "all in". All in means you are determined to pursue the dream with discipline, diligence and excellence. It means that you will not quit during tough times but will find solutions to every obstacle. Embrace your entrepreneurial power and commit. Once you make the pledge to yourself, and then tell family, friends and the world.

Building a business is not for the faint of heart, it requires commitment and hard work. It is a deliberate, progressive plan of action. It is a long journey that requires your full commitment but the benefits are well worth the ride.

It was character that got us out of bed, commitment that moved us into action, and discipline that enabled us to follow through.
Zig Ziglar

Examine your commitment to your dream and business goals. What are you most proud of? Is there room for improvement? Is it obvious that you are "all in" fully committed? Often we really believe in our dreams, yet we are hindered by fear or other obstacles that stop us from actively participating in the growth and development of that dream. Because of our constant conversations about the dream that are mistaken for commitment; we have no forward movement to build it. When examining your commitment, you should be focused and seek results.

When you are committed to a project, business or something, it is evident by your constant dedication to the bottom line, a victorious outcome. A committed mind is always looking for opportunities to improve, build and ultimately succeed.

    c. *Invest in you.* Dedicate time and resources to educate yourself and master your craft. An initial mistake we make is thinking that you must have all the necessary skills and resources to succeed from the beginning. That is not always true. However, you must constantly invest in you to have continual success. Invest time to learn new things, research opportunities and optimize resources.

    Successful people recognize that they can learn and grow from other people's stories, accomplishments and failures. Invest in training and development that will help you grow and become your best self. Educate you, change you and have fun doing it. Invest in your artistry and continue to empower and enlighten yourself. Grow your mind, see the possibilities. Remember, innovation comes from looking at the world with wonder and seeing the possibilities. You are worth the investment.

Invest in yourself. Your career is the engine to your wealth.
Paul Clitheroe

To build a successful business and accomplish your goals and objectives, you must strive to be your best self – mind, body and spirit. When you invest in yourself, you will grow and develop a better you. Here are a few self-investment ideas. Develop and nurture healthy habits. Build up inner discipline to make good choices. Get enough sleep. Preserve balance in your personal and business life. Exercise, rest and relax for a healthier you. Challenge yourself with personal goals. Create something new every day. Inspire yourself. Find a quiet space to reflect. Seek personal discovery.

>   d. *<u>Engage the support of others.</u>* Most successful people have mentors or coaches. A business mentor/coach is someone who is experienced, successful and willing to provide advice and guidance. Your business coach or mentor is someone you trust and are accountable to. Accountability and responsibility are basic tools for success. Engaging experts as mentors and coaches will be invaluable asset to your personal and business growth and development. Perhaps many of you have served in similar roles while providing support, empowerment and motivation to others.

>   Remember, you do not have all the answers. Never fail to be teachable; there is always something new

to learn. To build a successful business you must listen to people. Your customers, clients and others feedback will be priceless. Their feedback may either support your direction, cause you to reassess your decisions; and/or require you to make adjustments if necessary.

If you want to stand out as a leader, a good place is by listening. The best teams and bosses pay attention and value other's perspective.
Richard Branson

Be open to training, advice, criticism and support. Allow yourself time to think, create and listen. Be flexible. Think tanks, mastermind groups and other creative spaces are great resources especially for brain storming. A mastermind group is a highly motivated peer-to-peer monitoring group who share common business goals. They meet regularly to brainstorm, support and challenge one another. Building a business is hard work and it should be fun. If you do enjoy what you do and have fun doing it, what's the purpose? Build a business that engages and challenges others to enjoy making a difference.

 e. **_Build a strong support system._** Your support system is your initial dream team. Whether you start as a part-time entrepreneur, partnership or become a full-time business owner, you will need support. Remember, no man is an island. You will always need the support and assistance of others. As a startup, there are general proficiencies you will need to be successful; for example, an accountant, attorney, and administrative support. Based on your particular business or industry, you may require specialized skills to render your brand of services and/or products. One of your greatest and most valuable resources is your human resources -- your people. Engage and value them. As an entrepreneur and leader, your top priority is to align your strategy, people and operations. Therefore, you must acquire strong team building proficiencies.

Do not be afraid to engage the talents, gifts and strengths of other people. Partner with people who are stronger, better and wiser. According to Proverbs 27:17 - iron sharpens iron, means one man sharpens another. Join affiliations and other organizations to strengthen and assist your efforts and goals. Be smart enough to retain and/or employ the capacities, abilities and wisdom of others as needed.

Many successful businesses utilized family and friends to jumpstart their venture. Successful businesses have a supportive network of people to help fulfill the vision.

Remember, believe with your heart; with your mouth confess your faith! The principal thing is to believe in yourself and your dream. It sounds great, even doable; unfortunately, faith alone cannot generate results. It is amazing, even after we have accomplished much – we still deal with inner struggles and indecisiveness in times of transition or crossroads.

Yes, we believe and we are aware that we must take action to move forward. That is why; we must have a plan of action. For instance, believing that you can lose 20 pounds by your class reunion in the next 30 days is a wonderful goal. Unfortunately, it is just wishful thinking without an action plan.

Creating a well-written plan of action (for example, a weight loss plan) is insufficient without action "works". Francis Chan says it like this "true faith manifests itself in our actions". In other words, you must add work to your faith to make your dream a reality. To lose 20 pounds in 30 days will require work - exercise, diet changes and mental resolve. Just belief only is not enough – you must take action. Work your dream and make it your reality.

> *Faith is taking the first step*
> *even when you don't see the whole staircase.*
> Martin Luther King, Jr.

Turning Point Solution – *TAKE ACTION*

The move from dream to reality is to move from faith to action. Believe and walk by faith, and take the necessary actions to show your commitment. For many years, I really believed in my business dream and desired to be an entrepreneur. I shared my vision, hopes and dreams with friends and family. Encouraged and assisted others to start their businesses. Yet, my dream had not manifested itself because there was no specific work or action taken to make it a reality. One day I faced an unexpected crossroad called job displacement which caused me to reassess my future. This turning point pushed me towards my true purpose and I decided to start my first small business. It was exciting and intimidating all at the same time. After overcoming self-doubt and other distractions, I began to work my plan.

My first client was a former supervisor. From there I gained more confidence, additional clients and worked as a solopreneur for several years. In short, the shift from sleep walking through my dream to the manifestation of the building a business required action. Creating a living, breathing business requires hands on hard work and action. Once I began to work my faith, I achieved results. Focus, refocus add action and hard work to generate results and success.

Step Two – Make the Decision

Do something today that your future self will thank you for. Our actions and decisions today will shape the way we will be living in the future.
Unknown

Why make a decision? After acknowledging your belief in yourself and your dream, the next step is to make the decision to go forth. Making choices and decisions are a part of everyday life. At a pivotal crossroad, resolve to change your outcome. Every step of the way, we must make choices and decisions. Simply put, choices, choices, choices must always be made. Life presents hills and mountains, possibilities and challenges, opportunities and threats along the way that require you to make decisions. It is inevitable; you must choose. Choosing is exercising your right to action and exercising your right to freedom. Ask yourself, why make the decision? Answer, the decisions you make affect your destiny.

Making a decision to follow your dream requires change. Each choice you select demands a direction – go forth or go back. Clarity of what you want your future to be starts with a dream and then a confirmation of that dream. The initial decision to become an entrepreneur is to declare clearly this is your choice and plan for your life.

Every turning point calls for a response. Are you standing at a fork in the road? Are you at a transitional point in life? You must choose, right or left, forward or backward. The entrepreneur's call is alive and it is real. Every call demands an answer. It is a call to the entrepreneurial spirit in you. Dare to do it. Just say yes to the dream and next steps.

> *Your life changes the moment you make a new, congruent, and committed decision.*
> Tony Robbins

Some decisions are complex, others are easy, stressful or a combination of both. Often when you have decisions to make, you ask yourself questions. If money was not an issue and you could do whatever you want, what would you do? What is your dream life? Is it worth pursuing? Every passion, dream, or vision longs for fulfillment. Will you pursue? When? Perhaps, it is your dream that beckons daily, monthly, yearly and nothing happens because you never answered to the call. You have accomplished many things in life and overcome many challenges. You've done it before and you can do it now. See the possibilities. Redirect the energy of your frustrations and turn it into positive, effective, unstoppable determination.

Making a decision is the next step toward victory. Chose to follow your dreams and decide that turning back is not an option. You must internalize this confirmation: "My destiny is before me, my past behind me, no turning back, and no turning back".

> *Choices are the hinges of destiny.*
> Edwin Markham

Decide to build it, and then take action. Literally, making a decision sounds relatively easy because in your mind, you believe that you have already made the decision to start a business. You believe in the dream and believe in your ability to succeed. However, years have gone by and there is no noticeable or obvious forward progress. You know that making choices and decisions is a vital part of your daily and business life. Your journey through life has caused you to make some tough decisions, some excellent, some mediocre, others good and some bad. Yet, you still believe and dare to dream. The ups and downs, twists and turns, starts and stops required you to make choices and answer the questions: what, when, where and how. The lessons learned, experience earned made you wiser. Battle scars are only earned when you enter the battle.

So many folks are afraid of making the wrong decision that they make no decision at all. In fact, they actually made a decision to "do nothing". From our earliest memories as a child, we have had to make choices. Which cookie to choose, chocolate chip or peanut butter? Mom said you can only have one, so you must choose one or the other. Decision making means you must take responsibility for your actions and be accountable for your choices. Do not be afraid to own your decision. Believe in your power!

Decision-making forces you to examine the consequences, possible outcomes and financial or other related issues. Without being clear and decisive, you will have difficulty moving forward. Indecisiveness adversely affects your resolutions, solutions, judgment and conclusion.

Entrepreneurs must be bold, innovative, risk takers and courageous decision makers. Every path has two directions: up or down, left or right, back or forward. You must choose either one or the other. One may lead to success while the other may lead to the status quo – your safety zone. Standing still is not progress. You must choose one direction over the other to effectively change direction and change your life. Remember, failure is not fatal. Answer the call and prepare to change.

It doesn't matter which side of the fence you get off on sometimes. What matters most is getting off.
You cannot make progress without making decisions.
Jim Rohn

1. Prepare to Transform

You always have a choice, even when it is difficult to make a decision. In the end, you usually have only two choices – go backward or move forward. Standing still is a choice which will require additional action later unless you plan to standstill forever. Stop standing at the crossroads looking at your future through "what if". Take a leap of faith and decide to do it.

Clarity is so powerful. Indecisiveness is a stumbling block. Decisive and clear choices open the doors for change and transformation. If you have chosen to begin your entrepreneurial life or decided to transition from employee to a full-time business owner – then you are on your way; change is the platform for this movement.

Change is unavoidable and a natural transition in life's journey. Change is powerful and renewing. Change is the beginning of a new life, growth and new possibilities. Real change may make you uncomfortable. It changes your comfort zone. Dare to grow. Expand your horizons.

If we are growing we are always going to be outside our comfort zone.
John C. Maxwell

Transformation is not easy, especially if you do not yield or commit to it. As a part-time business owner or future entrepreneur, conversion is necessary to reach your ultimate goals. Remember, insanity is doing the same thing every time and expecting a different result. Expand your horizons. Be your best self. Exceed your expectations!

Start a new business; advance your current position. To accelerate you, your business or dreams will require change. To have effective change does not always require major renovations or significant investments. We can reach the top of the mountain one step at a time. You are allowed to rest, reorganize and plan along the way.

Real transformation starts in the mind. The change I want to see must first begin with me.

After many years of working as an employee and a part-time sole proprietor, you realized you have one repetitive dream – to be a full-time entrepreneur. Regardless of what changed in your life, regardless of the failures and successes at the end of your day, your heart says "I am a visionary".

Transformation brings clarity and self-motivation. Once you are clear who you are, you can roar: "I am an entrepreneur, an innovator, a creator, a dreamer who is unable to cease from dreaming. I was born to dream and cannot turn it off. I have decided to follow my dreams, one at a time." Immediately after gaining such clarity, you confirm your choice and state: "I'm all in." Once you commit, you solidify your transformation. Yes, embrace it. Evolve you; fulfill your vision.

As mentioned earlier, when you believe in something, you will invest in its growth and development. Like parents, entrepreneurs see the potential of their brain child and decide to invest their time, money and other resources to ensure that the vision prospers.

2. Change your mind

The entrepreneurial spirit is not something you are taught; it is something you must develop within yourself. Your mindset is your attitude, belief and habits. What you think affects what you do. If you plan to succeed, your thoughts should reflect that goal. If you think about success, then your actions, goals and objectives should be aligned with your desire to succeed in business.

If you like what you have accomplished but want to go higher, it requires more change. If you do not like where you are currently, you must change. Change is the ability to transform, modify or revolutionize someone or something.

> *We cannot become what we need by remaining what we are.*
> John C. Maxwell

The greatest resource you have is your mind. Empowering your mind creates growth and development that opens door for innovation and change. Intellect, brainpower and mental strength are tools of a change agent. As entrepreneurs, we are creative innovators who desire to change our world.

To change your mindset – approach or way of thinking – requires advance movement. Renew your mind with the possibilities. Refresh your mind with new ideas. Replace negativity with positive thinking.

Winners do not win because they are winners. They win because they believe. Winning is a mindset and approach to life. You already have what you need inside of you. Be positive. Be bold; lead by example. Push past the challenges and obstacles. Winners may fail but they get back up again. Do not be afraid to listen to the small voice inside.

A positive attitude causes a chain reaction of
positive thoughts, events and outcomes.
It is a catalyst and it sparks extraordinary results.
Wade Boggs

Remember, the person you are now is not who you will remain. You are evolving into the person you are destined to be. Perhaps, the caterpillar always dreamed of flying. The absence of wings never diminished his dream. A one-day transformation caused a miraculous change. Inside of him was always the ability to fly. He just needed to transform. A wondrous change yielded a beautiful butterfly. Do not be afraid of change, it is the evolution of new life. Embrace change, embrace your destiny. Do not underestimate the power of positive thinking and discipline. Well thought out plans are composed of good habits, meticulous practices and positive thinking.

3. Make a conscious decision.

Answer the call in the affirmative. Say "yes" to your dream of entrepreneurship; become a business owner or author, whatever you dream of, say "yes" to the transition from employee to employer. Start developing a plan for your transition. Decisiveness is difficult when you look at the obstacles you may face. When you make the decision and choice to become an entrepreneur, you have chosen a new path. Saying "yes" is a definite, affirmative action. Be the change you want to see. Now, you are an entrepreneur. Purpose to grow daily. Be wiser, stronger and better. Make the commitment to grow daily.

Once you decide to answer "Yes" every other action that you take should support your answer. From this point your actions should be intentional. Your lifestyle, mindset, mentors, habits and so on should support the fulfillment of the dream. Now let's move from the dream to the reality.

Your thoughts, reasoning and ideas should guide your actions to achieve goals necessary to move the business forward and upward.

> *All that a man achieves and all that he fails to achieve is the direct result of his own thoughts?*
> James Allen

4. Change your direction

Why change directions? Success always requires action and upward development. When you want to go higher and build bigger, you have to change directions. A new direction is necessary if you want to advance from your current position to one that is greater. Whether it is a promotion on the job, a new business strategy, or starting a new business, you must focus to change to reach a new target.

> *As we travel to new places we gain new perspectives and renew our thinking.*
> Lailah Gift Akita

a. Be bold and courageous

Remember, you are not required to change all at once. You are required to be brave enough to make small changes one day at a time. Dare to be bold and confident in the choices that you make. To be bold, you must believe in your unique greatness. Expect to exceed your expectations. Do not take no for an answer. Be your best self. Be brave; find better solutions.

b. Take Deliberate Risk

Entrepreneurs are risk takers. Take chances. Being a risk taker does not mean that you are irresponsible, unprepared or uninformed. Risk is a normal element of business. Notice, it is calculated risk that we exercise. Be prepared. You must always perform due diligence and thoroughly evaluate the pros and cons before making an investment. Do your homework.

c. Be Optimistic

Maintain a positive attitude about your future, your dreams and plans. Dare to dream big. Your vision should exceed your present hopes and expectations. Strive to be positive. Be confident. See the glass half full and seek to run it over. Inspire yourself; inspire others. Do something creative daily. Perform a random act of kindness for others. Hope for a better future.

d. Be Passionate.

What are you passionate about? What do you dream of doing? What problems will you solve? Passion is an essential "must have" characteristic of an entrepreneurial spirit. Passion is the driving force. It is the hunger, desire and thirst to build something great from nothing. Authentic, genuine passion energizes a true visionary. For example, you have a vision to build a business and become a strategic business coach. Your passion is to empower and encourage other aspiring entrepreneurs to get started, hurdle obstacles and build their businesses. Do what make your heart sing? When you are truly passionate about something, people can hear your conviction in your voice. When you believe with fervor, you speak with fiery passion.

Passion makes people go on to do exceptional things. If you believe in the dream, be passionate – push yourself to the limits to achieve it. Passion forces you to share your vision anytime you have an opportunity. If your heart is not in it, perhaps you should not be doing it. But if you seriously believe and are ready for the long haul, start now.

e. Get Clarity.

Most new businesses provide solutions to specific problems. The entrepreneurs turn problems into solutions. They turn solutions into opportunities. Before you can identify the solution, you must clearly recognize the problem. Where is the point of pain? What caused the problem?

Clarity is the essential thing. The visionary must have clarity to create a distinct, valuable and unified system. It allows the dreamer to see the vision and mission plainly. A clear perception permits the entrepreneur to see the whole, the entire system. Move from your purpose, to the problem, and to the solution. When you move in this manner, you will serve others by providing remarkable goods and services.

Yes, it is the key ingredient to creating a successful business system. Clarity of every integral part is vital before you can build it. First, you must know who you are. To your own self be true. Before you can commit and serve others, you must commit and serve yourself. Ask yourself – who am I? What is my purpose? Who are my customers? What is my competitive advantage? Without clarity you will waste valuable time and resources.

It is impossible to create change, lead change and buy-in if you do not know who you are. To be successful, you must know who you are and who you will serve, it is foremost. Basically, if you do not know your purpose, how will you fulfill it and help others? Lack of clarity will cause much frustration, possible failure and confusion. Know you. Know your purpose. Know your ideal customer/client. Are you clear?

Answer your entrepreneurial call; make the decision to fulfill your dream and purpose.

5. **<u>Reinvent You.</u>** Some turning points in life are perfect opportunities to reinvent yourself. In contrast, some life crossroads may be invasive and force us to make definitive choices when we would prefer not to deal with a particular situation at all. Nonetheless, some of our most challenges or toughest periods in life have compelled us to transform and/or reinvent ourselves through wiser, more grateful and self-revealing eyes.

During this wonderful growth surge of baby boomers, women and millennial entrepreneurs, many of those displaced in the job market, financially unprepared to retire, or dealing with huge college education debt find this season a great opportunity to reinvent themselves to capture their entrepreneurial spirit. While others just decided to seize the moment and follow their dream.

Once you have answered the call, now you can begin to tear down obstacles and begin to build, create or do whatever is in your heart to develop.

Life is a matter of choices, and every choice you make makes you.
　　　　　　　　　John C. Maxwell

Step Three – Overcome Obstacles

What hinders you? Obstacles are unavoidable aspects of everyday life. They are real hindrances and real distractions that have the potential to prevent or stop your progress. Obstacles are hurdles that you must jump over or overcome to continue moving forward. There is no victory without challenge. True success arises from opposition. To succeed you must overcome challenges and threats.

Even with a well-planned strategy, you will face known and unexpected obstacles. The first key to overcoming obstacles is to recognize that they are inevitable (expected, foreseeable, certain, and unavoidable). There will always be obstacles – issues, circumstances or reasons to quit. Once you acknowledge that they are a part of life's journey; then you can move on. Pause, breathe and regroup. Evaluate and reevaluate the situation thoroughly. Face your giants head on. Be courageous. Do not fear. Remember, giants do fall. Mountains can be moved.

For most Olympians, an obstacle is a temporary complication, barrier or hindrance that they must hurdle. Jump over, run around or tunnel through it. You must acknowledge it before you can defeat it. You cannot ignore them; they will not simply disappear. Be brave, forge ahead and make a decision to overcome your problem. To continue on your path, you must effectively deal with the obstacle face to face.

At every major turning point or crossroad, you can expect to face obstacles in your personal and business life. There are so many obstacles that you might face but there are three major obstacles that we have chosen to address. The order that these obstacles are in is important because the first obstacle directly impacts the others. .

> *Do not judge me by my successes; judge me*
> *by how many times I fell down*
> *and got back up again.*
> Nelson Mandela

The three major obstacles we may all face are self, fear and procrastination. Let's examine them, the impact on our decisions and choices; and how to overcome their negative influences.

1. **The biggest obstacle you will face is "You"**. Do you have a dream that you revisit in your mind over and over again? You shared it with family, friends and anyone willing to listen for years; yet, you have

"failed to launch" the vision. Ground zero has become a comfort zone. You have no written plan or you have written the plan but failed to execute it. No action, no movement. Sound familiar?

Why are you your own biggest obstacle? Pause and think about it. You are driven and/or hindered by what you think, believe and do. Thus, your biggest obstacle is in your "mind". What you think and believe, automatically affects what you do. If you constantly envision creating, doing and building something, then, why don't you do it? Ask yourself why. Have you allowed your personal fears to hold you hostage? Fear of failure and procrastination will hinder you.

Often you are your own worst enemy, not others. One day, you are full of inspiration and belief. The next day, you allow self to talk you down from the proverbial "leaf of faith". You use the lack of resources, time, money and anything else to either stop you or justify your slow down and lack of progress. Do not feel bad. It is human nature to doubt. Everyone at some point allows self-doubt, insecurities and fear to overtake them and influence their decisions. Some of the greatest heroes doubted themselves. Their power to overcome obstacles is evidence of their success as verbalized in each quote. They overcame by the power of their testimonies. Their stories can empower your story and your story will empower others.

Your comparison of your successes to others can hold you hostage. When you minimize your abilities, you become a barrier that hinders the fulfillment of your dreams. These are obstacles that taunt your mind. You must take control of them. Only you can. You are well able to overcome them. As stated in chapter one, you must first believe in yourself. Believe in your power.

You and you alone are responsible for your successes and failures, no one else. You hold the keys to unlock the vision and overcome every obstacle. Use your inner strength. Everything you need to succeed is inside of you. In you are seeds of greatness.

Believe in yourself, your abilities and your own potential.
Never let self-doubt hold you captive.
You are worthy of all that you dream of and hope for.
Roy Bennett

Remember how excited and driven you were after attending an empowerment conference where the room was filled with other dreamers, visionaries and innovators. You left believing that you could accomplish absolutely anything.

Nothing was impossible. You were on the path to victory – nothing could stop you now. What happened? Dreamer, what or who hindered you? What did you accomplish?

For years, you have encouraged and helped others reach their goals. You believed in their dreams and pushed them to victory. Many seek your advice and appreciate the gift that you are. They are waiting for the manifestation of your dream and will gladly follow you. How often do you captivate listening ears when you share your dream or vision? They will testify of your greatness. That is why - some of our students have excelled us. Their belief in our power exceeded our faith in ourselves. See, you do have power to change lives.

    a. **<u>It is not all about you</u>**. You hinder the fulfillment of your life's purpose when you think it is all about you. You are here to make a difference. Your passion, talents and abilities are gifts to the world. Someone you idolized caused you to believe in your power – was it a teacher, parent, or celebrity? Share your gifts and make a difference. You can change lives. Be the difference you want to see. Create the solutions to problems you have faced. Allow your crossroads to be a bridge for others. Dare to share your talents with the world!

You hinder your growth and potential when you allow fear to bind you. Freedom is the ability to make mistakes and learn from them. Freedom means that you are honest with you. Do not hide your talents under a bush. Learn to celebrate and share them. You are unique and one of a kind. There is no one exactly like you. Your purpose in the world is absolutely yours. How you chose to use your gifts and talents will determine your success.

> *We must believe that we are gifted for something,*
> *and that this thing,*
> *at whatever cost, must be obtained.*
> Marie Curie

b. **Think positively**. Examine what you habitually think, believe and do. If you believe that you are indeed the captain of your fate, then you must intentionally focus and direct your working energies toward your goals. Winners win on purpose. Do not allow doubt, fear of inadequacies to delay your plans. Whenever negative thoughts plague your mind, think positively. Motivate yourself with positive thoughts to change your mind. Encourage yourself. Speak words of affirmation aloud. Substitute negative thoughts with positive thinking.

Successful entrepreneurs are fearless, self-starters, self-motivated, pioneers and visionaries. Do they encounter challenges? Yes. Does fear, doubt, and other negative thoughts attack their minds? Of course, they do. Successful over-comers are persistent and determined to change their attitudes in order to win. Past accomplishments are reminders of your strength.

> *Once you replace negative thoughts with positive ones you'll start having positive results.*
> Willie Nelson

Only you can allow insecurity, doubt and indecisiveness to hinder you from living your dream life. Negative thoughts, words and attitudes justify your desire to quit before you start. Self-doubt and comparing yourself to others is self-destructive and can cause you to abort your dream before you even start to build it. Stop doubting yourself. Trust your instincts. Do not allow past failures to hinder future progress. Use failures as learning curves. Allow your past and current accomplishments to be a launching pad for greater things. If you believe it, speak it, and then do it.

2. Procrastination is the second major obstacle.

Why is procrastination an obstacle? Statistically, successful, high achievers and winners are historically characterized as driven people. They are men, women and young people motivated by the challenge or prize. Age, nationality or gender is not a factor – ask any of the top Olympians, i.e. Florence Griffith-Joyner, Mark Spitz, Jesse Owens, Michael Phelps, Paavo Nurmi or Usain Bolt. To complete the task or challenge necessary to win; they developed a plan of action and steadfastly followed the routine to ensure their success. Routines and plans are essential to develop good habits for success especially self-discipline. For example, every Olympian is highly disciplined in body, mind, thought, spirit and workouts to reach his goal. Discipline can be equaled to power. It is self-control, the ability to choose wisely using good judgment to bring balance in every area one's life while reaching ultimate goals. It is will power and restraint necessary to fulfill your goals and objectives.

What is procrastination? Procrastination is the practice of doing pleasant, easier and more rewarding tasks first in lieu of difficult more challenging tasks. It is defined by the American Heritage Dictionary as "to put off doing something, especially out of habitual carelessness or laziness". Procrastination is when you consistently delay particular tasks in lieu of less demanding or stressful assignments. It is postponing despite the belief that it may cause an adverse reaction or undue stress. Are you noticing the central theme? Habit is the key. In short, it is a bad habit working against your future. It is a belief that you always have more time and can do it later. Procrastination is disrespect for time.

> *Chains of habit are too light to be felt*
> *until they are too heavy to be broken.*
> Warren Buffett

Procrastination is a thief that comes to steal and kill your productivity and ambition. It is the decision to put off doing what needs to be done. It complicates your choices by influencing your decision to exercise will power or procrastinate. The choice to do something later minimizes the priority of the task at hand as well as the impact of your decision.

It is postponing despite the belief that postponing will cause an adverse reaction or problem. In short, it is a bad habit that can lead your failure. Bad habits can be broken.

As humans, our actions are directly and routinely influenced by our beliefs, attitudes and habits. Your beliefs are based on what you believe and/or perceive as the truth. And your attitudes are characteristics that reveal your personality, mood, and state of mind. Your behavior is the way you perform, work, operate and function. The culmination of your belief, attitude and behavior generates either good or bad habits. Habits are a part of who we are, like it or not. If procrastination is a bad habit, remember habits can be changed. You can change your habits and directly impact your future.

The misuse of time can be a deal-breaker for investors, customers and others. A healthy appreciation of time and how it impacts your business, personal life and others is invaluable. Successful people value time and its power to produce positive results.

Breaking bad habits requires a great deal of self-control. "Research indicates that it's worth the effort, as self-control has huge implications for success." Entrepreneur, Habits, October 2016

Winners always finish the race regardless of adversity. Whether you come in first, last, or somewhere in between, winners finish. Quitting is not an option. Quitters never win.

a. **Think about it?** How much time do you spend reading entrepreneur magazines, self-help or helpful tips about your chosen field of expertise or business? How much time do you spend on activities that do not add value to your life, business or future? We lose valuable hours watching TV or movies and doing other things that distract us from investing in your business or yourself.

If allowed to reign, procrastination may damage your creditability or reputation if you fail to meet major deadlines or obligations. Remember, it is a thief and robber of time and opportunity. What you think and do on a daily basis will either support or sabotage your business plans and dreams. You must choose to win. You must fight to win. You must change to be better!

We must use time as a tool, not as a couch.
John F. Kennedy

b. **Respect Time**. Time is an invaluable resource. You do not know how much time you really have. Use your time wisely; produce when and while you can. Do it on purpose. Remember, procrastination is the disrespect of time and its power to transform people, events and the world. It is the belief that you always have more time, so delay is always an option. Over time, walking in this belief develops into the bad habit of procrastination. It is the misappropriation of other people's time and the mismanagement of your time.

> *My favorite things in life don't cost any money.*
> *It's really clear that the most precious*
> *resource we all have is time.*
> Steve Jobs

A true visionary never stops dreaming. It is impossible to stop dreaming when you were born to create, produce and develop something. When you understand the pain of procrastination and decide to create solutions so others will not have to live with similar loss. You will create Turning Point Solutions, a remedy, strategic system to guide and support up and coming entrepreneurs at crossroads in their lives make the decision to leap into their dream life. Yes, you can continue to dream fresh ideas and overcame procrastination, fear and your personal hindrances to build and create. We can do it; you can too. If you can do it; others can, too.

You cannot regain lost or abused time. Yesterday's lost time cannot be restored. Activities and duties unaccomplished in the past must be completed using the present or future timeframes. Do not allow this to continue to hinder you. Release the past. Do not grieve over spilled milk. Start fresh today; work on developing new and better habits. Make breaking the power of procrastination a daily priority. If you have decided to fulfill your dream; plan to do it. Take action, work hard and seize the current moment. See each new day as another opportunity to make a change, fulfill your dreams and change your future. Realize each new day yields many possibilities.

Below are some basic tips for overcoming procrastination. In addition, you will need to be determined to succeed, build up self-control and work hard to more towards your ultimate goal one day at a time.

Tips for Overcoming Procrastination

1. **Get up early. Start fresh.** (make time to exercise, think and prepare)

2. **Focus.** (embrace and respect time). It is a gift and must be treasured.

3. **Set goals** (set short-time and long-term). Sacrifice pleasure for opportunity. Delayed is not denied, it is a choice.

4. **Create a daily "short" to do list.** Use only 1 to 3 items. Be specific.

5. **Prioritize** dedicated time. (Create by order - family, income generation, self...)

6. **Recognize or identify your triggers** – what distracts you? (Eliminate them immediately. Do not delay.)

7. **Avoid becoming overwhelmed.** (What makes you nervous, anxious, etc.? Why?)

8. **Make an assessment** at the end of each day. What happened, what did you accomplish, etc.? Do not quit.

Our life is the sum total of all the decisions we make every day, and those decisions are determined by our priorities.
Myles Munroe

Turning Point Solution – *Overcome Obstacles*

Have you ever attended an empowerment conference, mastermind group or business boot camp? Like me, do you remember how excited and driven we were after attending an empowerment conference where the room was filled with other enthusiastic dreamers, visionaries, innovators and entrepreneurs? I left believing that I could accomplish absolutely anything. Did you? Nothing was impossible. I was on the path to victory – nothing could stop me now. What happened dreamer? Slowly the excitement and motivation dissipated because I had not change my thinking, bad habits or other hindrances.

I continued to allow myself, procrastination and the fear of failure speak negativity in my heart and mind. Dreamer, what hinders you? Is your dream deferred? Langston Hughes says "a dream deferred is a dream denied". However, if we believe in our dreams and apply actionable faith, we can revive them.

Often, our desires alone are not enough to jumpstart our dreams, when self, procrastination or fear hinders us. We must deliberately plan to change our behavior and habits. This will require planning and execution. To overcome obstacles you must, like the Olympian, diligently study and understand your enemy and with much discipline make the necessary changes to transform yourself into a winner.

Above are some of the steps used to break the bad habits, stay focus and build more disciplined habits. Every day,

> I open and close each day for inspirational music and readings to validate my start and finish. Find what inspires and motivates you and develop your personal plan. Plan to succeed on purpose!

3. **Fear is our third and final obstacle**. The power to overcome any threat is to first recognize and clearly identify what it is. Therefore, let us define fear to better understand how to overcome it.

What is fear? Fear is defined as *an unpleasant emotion caused by the belief that someone or something is dangerous, likely to cause pain, or a threat*. Fear derives its power and ability to hold you captive from your belief that it is real and it can conquer you. Your belief causes you to believe that the adverse consequence, pain or threat generated from fear will be detrimental, unbearable or dangerous.

As mentioned earlier, your beliefs are based on what you believe and/or perceive as the truth. And, your attitudes are characteristics that reveal your personality, mood, and state of mind. The culmination of your belief, attitude and behavior toward someone or something you fear may generate negative emotions, thinking or habits. It is not my intention to undermine the reality of fear in your life should not be undermined. The sole objective for dealing with the distraction of fear is strictly related to its impact on business ownership perspective and decision making.

Today, we live in a world with terrorisms, diseases and other threats that may devastate our personal and business world. However, it is my goal to remind you how extremely resilient and powerful the human mind is. We can overcome all adversity. We can manage all perceived fear. We have the ability to restore and renew our minds. We can change our way of thinking. We can choose to think positive.

When fear captivates you, it impacts your attitude and thoughts toward something as well as your habits. For example, if you believe you will fail in business and quit before you start, fear won. You have allowed fear, without any real evidence that you cannot succeed in business by aborting your plans in advance. This we call the fear of failure. You actually quit before you start.

Overcoming fear is the first step to success for entrepreneurs.
The winners all exemplify that,
and the hard work and commitment they have shown
underlines what is needed to set up a business.
Richard Branson

1. The Fear of Failure

Fear is false evidence appearing real. Fear of failure is a hindrance to launching a successful plan. Often the fear of failure will cause you to unconsciously sabotage your chances of success. Fear is a very real emotion and response to real threats. When you are overcome by fear, you are usually threatened by the possibility of an adverse or negative outcome before it actually happens. The possible outcome is false evidence, yet it appears to be real. In most instances, you cannot predict the outcome.

If failing is the worse you can do, then decide that you will fail trying to succeed. For when you succeed, you will have succeeded failure. In reality, the worse you can do is quit before you start. In this instance, you have allowed your fear of failure to paralyze you without executing the plan. Do not abort your brainchild before giving birth it and allowing the vision to manifest itself.

The fear of failure can directly affect your business. When you are so frightened of failure, it may impact your decision making or risk-taking abilities. Often, we can clearly identify the fear of failure when you consistently find reasons to either delay moving forward or reasons why we cannot build or succeed, at all.

Fear of failure and fear of the unknown are always defeated by faith. Having faith in yourself, in the process of change and in the new direction that change sets will reveal your own inner core of steel.

Georgette Mosbacher

Fear of failure may be big, bold and ugly, or simply disguised as the fear of social media, public speaking or sales negotiations. Here, the fear of rejection is directly related to the fear of public speaking and sales negotiations. As a result of these fears, we may consistently avoid or dislike the vital tasks to our business growth and sustainability.

The only guarantee for failure is to stop trying.
John C. Maxwell

2. Do not be afraid to F.A.I.L

Do not feel guilty if you do not win every challenge. Failing is a natural part of success. The reality is you will have some failures. Embrace your failures. Learn from them. There are always valuable lessons to learn from every experience; the good, bad and ugly are teachable moments. Have you ever allowed fear of failure or fear of success halt your progress? What would happen if you persevered and overcame your fear of failure; success is definitely a viable option? Do not fear failure.

> *If you fail, never give up because F.A.I.L. means "First Attempt in Learning" ...*
> Dr. Abdul Kalam

The only way to prevent failure is to stop trying. If quitting before you start is not an option, then you must pursue your vision with determination. You do not have to win every battle to win the war. Plan to succeed. If your first attempts fail, step back, regroup and start again. Planning is a process that benefits from learning curves. Remember, failure is not fatal unless you abandon the plan and quit.

You conquer fear when you allow your faith in yourself and your vision to exceed your fear. Prepare, plan. Organize, get ready. Master your craft. Train, practice. Believe in yourself. Believe in your dream. Be coachable and teachable. Be bold, courageous and work your plan.

> *Let your faith be greater than your fear.*
> Anonymous

3. Embrace failure's learning curve

Assess and acknowledge the best outcome and worse scenario. "Do not be embarrassed by your failures, learn from them and start again" Richard Branson. Experience is the best teacher, if you chose to learn from your mistakes. It would be wonderful if you, the entrepreneur reached your ultimate potential and maximized your investment on the first attempt. Unfortunately, it is unrealistic to expect to be an overnight wonder. Dream on, but if at first you do not succeed, try, try again. Examine the track records of other successful entrepreneurs and innovators before you; you will discover that the majority of them have a list of failures before they succeeded.

I learned that courage was not the absence of fear, but the triumph over it.
The brave man is not he who does not feel afraid, but he who conquers that fear.
Nelson Mandela

You can move forward or quit now. Now decide which you choose to do, succeed or fail. You have the power to choose. Then learn to get over yourself. Failing is neither an option nor a choice but a reality of business. Most successful entrepreneurs have experienced failure. Focus on what you can control. Release aspects that are not in your control. The ability to choose is empowering. Always chose to use your power. Shake yourself off, pick yourself up and continue to take calculated risks and proceed to win.

If you chose to, you can overcome any obstacles. Because you have chosen to win in life and business, you cannot quit. You must accept the fact that you may fail sometime but failure cannot define you. You do not have to win every battle but you are determined to win the war for your dream life. You will plan to succeed and not to fail. Chose success, it is obtainable. Now let's hurdle fear, move forward and write the vision.

Focus on where you want to go, not on what you fear.
Tony Robbins

Step Four – Write the Vision

You may think that starting a business is hard. Indeed, it is but it is also attainable. Yes, it requires hard work, discipline and commitment. No, it is not easy but it is rewarding and achievable. Unfortunately, many fail because they never start. Too many aspiring entrepreneurs get stuck early in the process because they think only a certain type of people have what it takes. The reality is most people have what it takes but only a few chose to do it. What most people lack, however, is the patience, determination and ability to plan for success.

Yes, you must plan and prepare to succeed. It is easy to become overwhelmed in the early stages of starting a business. You must prepare for the long haul. One key is to have a well prepared written vision. The most important "why" to answer is your reason for starting your business. Get major clarity for your reason. Whatever your reason: being your own boss, creative expression, being home with the kids or helping others – knowing what drives your passion will keep you focus and committed to the dream not matter the circumstances.

At each significant turning point in life, you need a clear path to follow to the next phase of your journey. It is impossible to make wise decisions without a visual of the possibility or expected end. The vision is specific, is goal-oriented and has benefits for others. To arrive at your expected end, you must have a clear cut roadmap for the journey. The written business plan is your roadmap.

Where there is no vision, there is no hope.
George Washington Carver

1. Write the vision

Why is it important to write down your vision? The written word is a powerful articulation of the vision. It speaks volumes to the reader. It directs, empowers and reinforces our resolve to do something. Have you ever read a book that changed your life? Or an article that caused you to make a life change? The written word you read had power because it personally spoke to you; it said exactly what you needed to hear. It spoke life to your future and provided confirmation to guide your next steps. Words have power.

A written vision provides clarity, direction and empowerment. It allows you to capture words of inspiration and wisdom for future implementation. The written dream helps the dreamer to visualize it, build it and execute a plan of action. "Without a vision, the people perish." Why do the people perish without a vision? Because they do not have a clear and precise roadmap to reach their goal – the promise land. The written vision is your roadmap to the manifested dream. It is your guide from the vision to reality.

A well-detailed documentation of your vision can provide a graphical guide to follow. Your mission/purpose will help you to navigate through well planned goals and objectives that will lead to the reality of your creation – your dream business, invention, new lifestyle, etc. When moments of clarity and inspiration happen, a written vision allows you the opportunity to revise and fine tune the finished project.

The written vision allows you time and space to exercise your creative power. It provides an opportunity to revisit the message and make adjustments along the way. The written word allows you to see the living dream, visually. It reveals the possible reality. It helps you to see it before you actually see it. You see it in your mind's eye before you see it with your natural eye. The written word allows you to make the vision breathe and live. Create it on paper first. Write the vision; make it plain so he may run that reads it.

It is powerfully important for your audience to read it and be able to run with a clear understanding of what your business does and how it impacts others.

Seeing your goal written in ink, on paper will have a powerful effect on your mind.
Anonymous

2. Journalize it

Journalizing your vision, dream and all related thoughts is a must. Often inspiration appears when you least expect it. An awakening may be turned on by words in a song, a glimpse, or a conversation with a friend and it must be captured. Always carry a journal or notebook to document moments of inspiration, clarity and innovation. Vision develops over a period of time as you meditate on the processes to fruition.

You may want to place a vision book or note book next to your bed or special thinking place to capture every brainwave. Unfortunately, you do not remember every bright idea or sketch that flashes in your mind, so you must jot it down. Journalize to document momentarily gatherings of the whole. While the data is flowing continue to write. Do not stop to read or reread, write until you have completed the thoughts.

Journaling is an extremely powerful and resourceful tool. Writing is self-expressive. It allows you to capture your thoughts in written words. The more clarity you gain, the better you can communicate to others. You may have already discovered its invaluable ability to bring the vision to life. Such a tool should become part of your sustainability plan. This is an ongoing revelation of ideas, dreams and visions.

A dream written down with a date becomes a goal. A goal broken down into steps becomes a plan.
A plan backed by action makes your dreams come true.
Leon J. Suenes

3. Make it plain

Make it plain means to keep it simple, readily understandable and clear. Be specific – what is your purpose? What will you create? What will you build? Who will you help? How will you do it? What is your why? What solution will you provide?

Write down absolutely everything you think about your business plans. Document everything you plan to accomplish. Regardless of how big or small, record your thoughts. Take time to brainstorm and capture invaluable insight about your vision and business. Be precise, document your thoughts, goals, ideas, etc. Think about what you want your business to be a year from now and write it down. Be very specific Reread your vision daily, in the morning and evening. Focus of the end results.

4. Write the business plan.

There are two specific plans used to support your strategy- a strategic plan and the business plan. A strategic plan is primarily used for implementing and managing the strategic direction of an existing organization. It is used by established business as a map for three to five-year planning. Initially, a business plan is used to start a business, obtain funding, or direct operations. The two, strategic and business plans cover different timeframes as well.

To plan for success and articulate a clear plan of action, you must write a business plan. In the business world, the plan is your strategic map from conception to fruition. It should include your business concept, mission, vision, core values, goals, objectives and competitive advantage. It is a crucial decision making tool.

Being an entrepreneur means you are a big dreamer. Therefore, you must create short-term and long-term goals as well as big dream goals for the life of your business. This allows you to plan for long-term sustainability.

Your business plan is a powerful tool and if used properly can help you move forward, stay on track, and meet your goals. You should revisit your plan yearly and evaluate your business, changes to analyze growth, sustainability, increase in sales and diversification.

The following are the parts of a simple business action plan.

a. **Executive Summary** – write this last. It can be as short as one page and include the business highlights. Here you tell your reader where you are, where you want to go and why your business idea will be successful. Your executive summary will be more extensive if you are more established versus a start-up. If well established, you may include a company profile, mission, company growth, and other future plans.

b. **Business/Project Description**. State your vision, mission, history, start-up plans, and location of your business. Include your biography and statement - focus on your experience and background as well as the decisions that led you to create this particular business. Define your competitive advantage. What makes you unique? What makes you different?

c. **Services, Products and Pricing**. What gap or need do you address in the market? Why should people purchase your products or services? Identify streams of income and revenue opportunities.

d. **Marketing and Sales**. Launch marketing and brand-awareness campaigns. How do you plan to market your business? Build and communicate your brand.

e. **Goals and Objectives**. Your goals and objectives must be clearly defined, simple to administer and widely communicated and aligned with your mission, strategy, people and operations.

You will need short-term and long-term goals. List actionable tasks and steps necessary to accomplish them. Short-term may be up 1-2 years. Long-term should be 3-year and 5-year plans are a good start. Keep your goals simple. Use the helpful SMART strategy to create good goals and objectives. SMART goals setting is a tool that brings structure and tractability into your goals and objectives.

1. S – Specific
2. M – Measurable
3. A – Attainable
4. R – Realistic
5. T – Time-based

f. **Financial Projections**. Prepare the budgets. Demonstrate your potential. Generate financial projections to set targets, cash forecasts and other performance analyses. These projections provide valuable feedback for gauging progress and alignment with strategic plans. .

5. Create a 30-60 second elevator speech.

You should create a 30-60 second elevator speech. What is an elevator speech? Once you have mapped out your plan, use your executive summary to create your elevator speech. It is easier to condense the directions. You can provide a clear and concise short-cut to the expected end. This is your quick flash into your business and vision shared with potential customers, investors, partners, etc. Your elevator speech is a power tool to build your confidence, share your story and communicate your brand.

Another simple guide for planning and developing your business is as follows:

1. **Always take time to brainstorm**. Plan for every aspect of the business for various phases of time.

2. **Gather needed resources**. Assess your resources and potential needs, especially essential for startups.

3. **Get the finances in shape**. Setup a budget to accomplish your goals. Create short-time (one-two years) and long-term (three to five years) budgets for sustainability.

4. **Mobilize and engage people**. Staff, customers and partners are your people power. You must have involved, engage, empower and energize people to help fuel your business.

5. **Magnify your uniqueness**. Branding is a powerful tool. You must always ensure that you protect it, promote it and perform it.

6. **Activate and maintain clear lines of communication**. Ensure your mission and objectives are clearly communicated. Maintain an effective system for upward and downward communication

throughout your organization. Listen to your people, their words have power.

Your written plans will prove to be an invaluable tool when used properly and routinely to guide your business strategies. It must always be reviewed, analyzed and changed as needed to ensure continual success.

Now onward and upward to execute your action plan. Next step. Ready, set execute.

*I think that the greatest gift God ever gave man is
not the gift of sight but the gift of vision.
Sight is a function of the eyes,
but vision is a function of the heart.*

Myles Munroe

Step Five – Execute Your Plan

At this stage, you have already affirmed your belief in your dream and made the decision to answer the entrepreneur's call. You have chosen to conquer and overcome obstacles that have hindered you from moving forth. By exercising your faith in the dream's reality, you wrote the vision, mission, goals and objectives – the entire business plan. Now you are ready to implement your business strategies, engage your people and operate your business. Execute, simply means, get it done. According to Larry Bossidy and Ram Charan, the definition of execution is "the way to link three core processes of any business – the people process, the strategy, and the operating plan – together to get things done on time". Execution (follow through) is one of the greatest challenges you and all leaders will face, it is a disciplined practice. From the quotes of many great leaders, we can presume that the power to execute is a learned behavior and executive management skill.

Execution is one of the most difficult and challenging steps. Many entrepreneurs fail at executing the plan. Follow through is key to your business success. This is where the rubber meets the road. Step five requires great discipline and a relentless determination to get it done. Key words focus and results. Stay focus throughout the operating process to generate great results.

> *Strategy execution is the responsibility that makes or breaks executives.*
> Alan Branche and Sam Bodley-Scott, Implementation

Execute the plan is to start the ball rolling. The initial planning to help you visualize the dream starts with writing the vision and making it plain. Executing the plan is launching the goals, objectives and ideas to make the vision a reality and implement the operations. To execute the plan successfully, you must follow a strategic plan and systematic process, and engage your people.

The key to executing or implementing your strategy for success is to ensure the following:

1. **Communicate** – You must ensure that there is upward and downward communication. First, you must establish a system to engage your organization with two-way communication and establish a system for feedback. Communicate your vision repeatedly and mission to your team.

2. **Celebrate**. Always invest in your greatest resource, your people. Celebrate them, their investment, contributions and talents. Engage them.

3. **Commit**. Commit time, energy and resources strategically to strengthen your competitive edge and corporate synergy. Commit to your people – customers, staff and partners. Commit to branding. Commit to your movement.

4. **Collaborate**. Strategies, solutions and operating systems should be woven into the overall fabric of your business mapping. Alignment of operations, people and strategies is paramount. Build strong, cohesive teams. In fact, it is critical for long-term success and sustainability.

5. **Chase**. Track your performance. Review feedback. Pursue new ideas and opportunities. Always review and analyze your results.

The result of bad communication is a disconnection between strategy and execution.
Chuck Martin, former vice president, IBM

Ready, Set, Launch! Executing the plan is launching all prepared and planned operating systems to begin your business journey. Again, it requires an alignment of the three vital components: strategy, operating systems and people. Maintain consistent, clear and concise communication throughout the organization to ensure that the systems are working as planned or to determine if and when changes are necessary to correct errors and avoid significant failure, losses or downtime.

Regularly evaluate to ensure that you have the right people, resources and materials necessary to succeed. Whether your business is a day or a year old, continue to set goals, plan and analyze feedback in order to move your business forward.

Good business leaders create a vision, articulate the vision, and passionately own the vision,
and relentlessly drive it to completion.
Jack Welch

Without execution, "vision" is just another word for hallucination.
Mark V. Hurd

Turning Point Solution – *Follow Through and Seize the Moment*

Have you ever had a great idea and failed to follow through? Perhaps, you created or invented something or started a project. You believed in your dream and decided to move forward. You met with a patent attorney. Searched for patents and discovered it had not been created yet. No patent existed, early to the market. Free, clear and possible is your vision. Now it is time to develop the prototype. What an opportunity!

Perhaps, like me, that is how your story began. Yes, I believed in my dream and shared my vision with close friends and family. Years later, my dear friend calls screaming in distress because my invention was currently appearing on the television. I lost a golden opportunity to change my life, my family's and others' lives. I failed to seize the moment and someone else had a similar dream and executed their plan. This was a huge loss. What if I had seized the moment? What opportunities have you lost?

Somewhere between meeting with the patent attorney and the execution of my plan, life happened. There were several life-changing events that occurred one after the other – loss of a sibling, family health and financial issues. Surely, I could blame major life challenges as a good reason for failing to follow through and execute the plan. Life happens to all. Some events should change our directions and/or may interrupt our plans and progress. But was it the real reason I failed to seize the moment. No, it was not. First of all, I did not write out my vision or plan of action. As a result, I lacked clarity and direction. Then procrastination reared its ugly head and I functioned as if there was more time. Although, it was important, my actions indicated that it was not a high priority.

A loss of this magnitude was definitely a vital turning point and learning curve for me and a teaching moment that I frequently share with others. Remember, failure is not fatal. You can prevail and learn from your mistakes. However, it is imperative that we plan (write the vision) and execute the plan "get it done, no matter what". Without a plan, we plan to fail. In addition, we must identify our personal obstacles and overcome them. You must diligently work to change bad habits that may impact both your personal and business life.

> Don't lose sight of your dream and vision. You still have purpose and passion. A true visionary always dream. When you fail, don't faint, dare to dream bigger. Continue to build and create. Follow my steps: believe, decide, overcame, write the vision, plan and execute. Get it done! Seize the moment and Execute!

Ideas are cheap. Ideas are easy. Ideas are common. Everybody has ideas.
Ideas are highly, highly overvalued. Execution is all that matters.
Casey Nesitat

Step Six – Plan to Succeed

The sixth and final step to answering the entrepreneurial call and starting your business is *planning to succeed*. When you plan to succeed, you must have an expectancy of success. Failure is not an option. Neither failure nor disruptions are options if you plan to succeed. Believe, believe and believe you can. Intentionally purpose to succeed. Create a strategy to win. Plan wisely, plan systematically, plan optimistically and plan strategically. Basically, plan to succeed means to deliberately develop a business strategy that ensures a favorable outcome. It does not mean that you will not have distractions, challenges and/or losses. Plan, plan and plan again. Never fail to plan.

Success doesn't just happen. It's planned for.
Anonymous

Plan to Succeed means that after thoroughly analyzing your options, visualizing your dream, performing all relevant due diligence, you have chosen to win on purpose, not haphazardly, not by chance or by luck but because you have prepared, planned and chose to win. You are moving forward with eyes wide opened. Now, you are determined and committed to do what is necessary to accomplish your goals and objectives. You are all in.

> *"By failing to prepare, you are preparing to fail."*
> Benjamin Franklin

Now you firmly believe that it is your purpose to solve a particular problem that will change other people lives. You have taken the bull by the proverbial horns and plan to build a business.

After you have done everything you can to ensure success, stand firmly in your strengths, determination and commitment to see it through. You have wisely and fully dedicated time, efforts and resources and faithfully followed the well-documented plans and executed the systems to fulfill the company's goals and objectives.

> *Success demands singleness of purpose.*
> Gary Keller

> *Successful people are not gifted;*
> *They just work hard, then succeed on purpose.*
> Unknown

Eight keys for Planned Success

1. **Lead** with integrity
2. **Engage** your people
3. **Trust** your instincts
4. **Align** your strategy, people and operations
5. **Sow** into other people lives
6. **Learn** and always be teachable
7. **Execute** your plan with fervor
8. **Generate** and review feedback.

Entrepreneurship is not for the faint of heart. Many were told that they would never make it, and have exceeded their nay-sayers. Remember, wealth is not built overnight. Be hungry, always looking for a better way, another great idea. Keep your ears open, listen to your customers, staff and partners. Keep in mind, there is always room for improvement. Think bigger and better. Be innovative, think outside of the box.

One of the greatest lessons that we may discover during our entrepreneurial journey is the long-term power of discipline. Discipline is will power self-control to manage and direct one's developing good habits and routines. It is the ability to exercise restraint to accomplish specific goals and objectives. Discipline is one of the high achievers' tools of success. You see this truth in analyzing the challenges and successes of Olympians.

> Some succeed because they are destined to.
> But most succeed because they are determined to.
> Iliketoquote.com

> "Live the life of your dreams:
> be brave enough to live the life of your
> dreams according to your vision and
> purpose instead of the expectations
> and opinions of others."
> Roy T. Bennett

Conclusion

Here we are at the conclusion of six thought-provoking and motivational steps to jumpstart your entrepreneurial dream. Some of you have come to the end of the six step journey, and have decided to begin your business venture or fulfill your life's dream. Others are still contemplating whether it is the next movement for your life. Remember you are never too young or too old to dream and fulfill your vision. Life's journey is full of wonderment, choices and possibilities. We must all chose our own path. Everyone has a purpose and passion that defines your distinctive power. Our passions, dreams and visions drive us as we seek to fulfill our individual destiny. No matter how old you are, dare to follow your dreams.

A turning point may be a moment of self-discovery. For you can discover your authentic passion, power and purpose at any age and answer the call. Your destiny is at the center of your passion and power. Every dreamer is like a caterpillar, a wishful thinker until he/she transforms into a beautiful visionary with wings to fly and soar.

The author believes we were born to fulfill our distinctively unique purpose in life. Within each of us is the ability to create, build and transform. You were born to solve problems that will change lives and the world. We can learn from one another mistakes and successes. Our journey is full of challenges, victories, failures, regrets and successes. When we dare to share our story to help others, we can prevent them from making similar errors and ultimately move them closer to their destiny. Your stories can empower, strengthen and help others from facing the pitfalls and obstacles that we encountered on our road to destiny.

Can you surmise that your turning point is a divine pivotal moment in time created as a compass to direct your entrepreneur's path? You are the navigator; you must choose the course to follow. You must lead the way and manage every course of action. Ask yourself, "If money was not an issue and you could do whatever you want, what would you do"? Every passion, dream, vision and imagination longs for fulfillment. Dare to follow your passions. Will you pursue your dream?

The author is so grateful that many dreams continued to flutter our hearts, minds and souls. Despite our lack of commitment, lost opportunities, stagnation (possibly a result of fear, self-doubt and/or procrastination) and failure to launch; our dreams still live and awaits our actionable faith to manifest its reality. For many, your dream continues to thrive in every sleeping moment and whispers in every waking instant for fulfillment. Only you can answer your calling.

Are you compelled to answer your mission's call? Ordinary men and women answered their life's calling and were transformed into great leaders, visionaries and change agents. Some great dreamers begin as children or youth envisioning the possibilities; utilizing their youthful creativity to manifest innovative ideas. Unfortunately, there are many great and unfulfilled dreams that will die with their dreamers. Every dreamer must choose his/her own path. Which path will you choose?

How do you know if your mission in life is finished?
If you're still alive, it isn't.
Richard Bach

Today, we live in a very exciting, e-commerce business globe. The possibilities are constantly expanding with changes in technology. The number of new entrepreneurs and businesses are growing and expanding the competitive market. Forbes acknowledged significant growth by baby boomers, millennial and women entrepreneurs entering the marketplace. No matter who you are or where you are, the marketplace is open and anxiously awaits your new innovative ideas and businesses.

Our world is threatened by terrorisms, diseases and other pressures that may devastate our personal and business lives. However, it is my goal to remind you how extremely resilient and powerful we are. We can overcome all adversity. We can manage all perceived fear. We have the ability to restore and renew our minds. We can change our way of thinking. We can choose to think positive. In you is the ability to transform yourself and others by solving problems to some challenge. Embrace your passion! Fulfill your destiny and succeed on purpose.

May every dreamer be motivated and empowered to fulfill their purpose and find clarity, purpose and directions. Let today be the start of your entrepreneurial voyage with inspiration, empowerment and great expectation. May wisdom, power and people follow you as you seek to make a difference to better our world.

Every great advancement was once nothing more than a dream in the mind of a visionary.
Robin Sharma

NOTES

Introduction

The Book of Ecclesiastes 3: 1 (King James Version)

British & World English, Oxford Dictionary, https://en.oxforddictionaries.com/definition/turning_point

Stengel, Geri. (2016/01/06). Re: Why The Force Will Be With Women Entrepreneurs In 2016. *Entrepreneurs.com. Forbes/Forbes Woman*. Retrieved from https://www.forbes.com/sites/geristengel/2016/01/06/why-the-force-will-be-with-women-entrepreneurs-in-2016/#3ff0387d4f8b

Rogers, Kate. Thursday, (2017/05/04). Re: Boomer Entrepreneurs are making it big by doing what they love. *CNBC.com*. Retrieved from https://www.cnbc.com/2017/05/04/boomer-entrepreneurs-are-making-it-big-by-doing-what-they-love.html

Daisyme, Peter. (2015/05/06). Many Baby Boomers Are Choosing Entrepreneurship Instead of Retiring. *Entrepreneurs.com*. Retrieved from https://www.entrepreneur.com/article/245366

Oxford Dictionaries. Oxford University Press. Retrieved from https://en.oxforddictionaries.com/definition/solopreneur

Wikipedia. (2015) Retrieved from https://en.wikipedia.org/wiki/Sole_proprietorship

Step One

Hebrews 11:1 (Common English Bible)

Proverbs 23:7 (King James Version)

Clark-Sheard, Karen. *"It's Not Over"*. 2nd Chance. Karew Records, 2002. CD

Piper, Watty. (1930). *The Little Train That Could*. Chicago, IL. Platt & Munk.

Step Two

English/Oxford Dictionary. Retrieved from https://en.oxforddictionaries.com/definition/fear

Step Three

Bradberry, Travis, *(2016/10/25). Entrepreneur, Habits.* 10 Bad Habits You Must Eliminate from Your Daily Routine. Retrieved from https://www.entrepreneur.com/article/284214

Step Five

Bossidy, Larry, Ram Charan & Burck, Charles. (2002). Execution: *The Discipline of Getting Things Done.* Crown Business.

www.ingramcontent.com/pod-product-compliance
Lightning Source LLC
Chambersburg PA
CBHW070307230526
45470CB00002B/767